EASY SCOTTISH HARP MUSIC

MB21917
BY SHARON HANJIAN RONDEAU

Sharon Hanjian Rondeau

Sharon Hanjian Rondeau began the study of the harp at the age of eight with Dr. Aristid von Wurtzler at the Hartt School of Music, University of Hartford. Her first public performance was at the age of 9 on Channel 3 in Hartford as a member of the Hartt College Harp Ensemble and as a soloist.

She was a four-time consecutive winner at the Festival of Irish Culture in the Bronx, NY and won first place in the Junior Division of the American Harp Society national competition in 1969. In 1975 she was awarded a full scholarship to the Eastman School of Music to study with the renowned Eileen Malone.

Sharon has performed extensively throughout New England and New York, including a November 2004 performance with the University of Connecticut Studio Orchestra at Carnegie Hall. She is currently principal harpist with the New Britain (CT) and Manchester Symphony Orchestras. Her main focus, however, has been to showcase the concert harp as a versatile solo instrument, particularly in the area of Celtic music. Her "Celtic Reflections" CD, available at *www.harpinmotion.com*, contains her own interpretations of traditional English, Welsh, Scottish and Irish songs.

TABLE OF CONTENTS

Am Buachaille Ban (The Fair Shepherd)

Trad. Scottish, arr. SHR

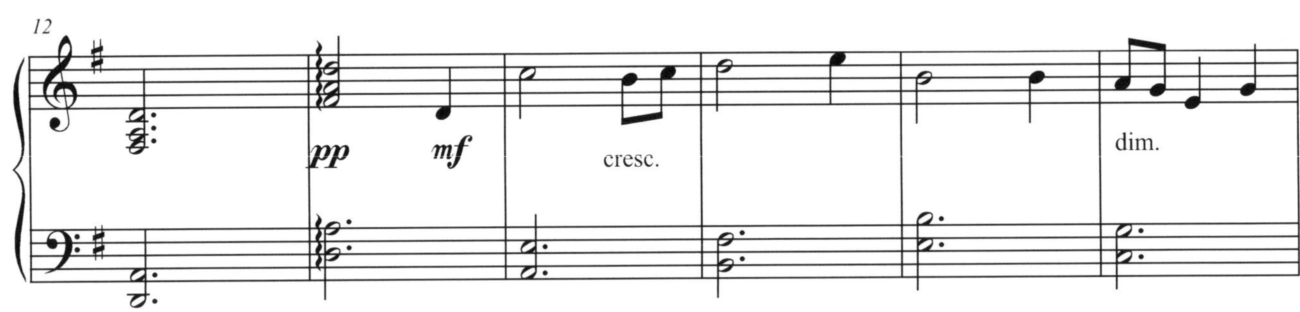

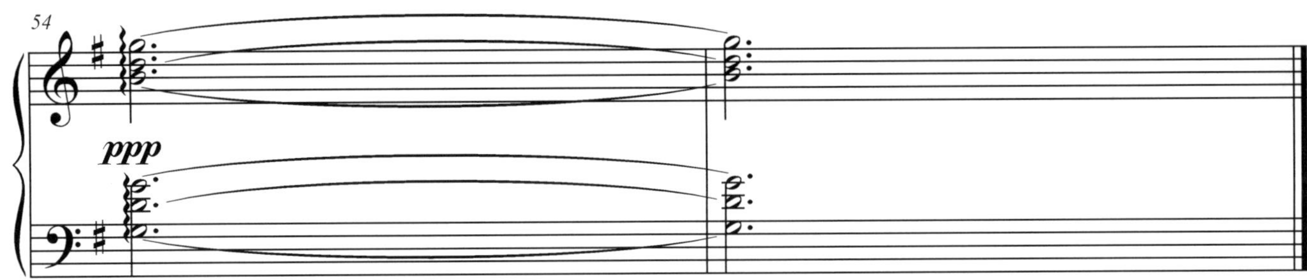
54
ppp

THE SLOPES OF STRATH BÀN

Walking out early alone on a morning in May among green fields, an outcast and purposeless, I saw a maiden who lived some way above me as she washed her clothes out on the slopes of Strath Bàn.

I then climbed upwards to the maiden I loved, and courteously and mildly I spoke to her: "It's over a year since our love began, and if you are willing, we shall marry at once."

"Marry? I'm too young to marry just now – your sort has a tongue that could cause trouble anywhere; my father and mother would scold me forever more if I were to marry the likes of you, you feckless young man."

But you young girls everywhere who are still unmarried, don't go turning young men down through pride or contempt. How sad for me to be unmarried forever more – I'll have to live alone, out on the slopes of Strath Bàn.

Aodann Srath Bhain (On the Slopes of Strath Ban)

Trad. Scottish, arr. SHR

8

Iainn Ghlinn' Cuaich (John of Glen Cuiach)

21
pp mf
decresc.
mp
rit.
26
p
pp

Kintail

Folk harpers tune 1st, 2nd & 3rd B♭

Simply and slowly

24
p
mf
30
rit. al fine
pp

Ma Theid Mise Tuilleadh (If I Ever Go Again)

Trad. Scottish, arr. SHR

rit.
decresc.
pp

NOW WESTLIN WINDS

Words by Robert Burns

Now westlin winds and slaughtering guns
Bring autumn's pleasant weather
The moorcock springs on whirring wings
Among the blooming heather.
Now waving grain, wild o'er the plain
Delights the weary farmer
And the moon shines bright as I rove at night
To muse upon my charmer.

The partridge loves the fruitful fells
The plover loves the mountains
The woodcock haunts the lonely dells
The soaring hern the fountains.
Through lofty groves the cushat roves
The path of man to shun it
The hazel bush o'erhangs the thrush
The spreading thorn the linnet.

Thus every kind their pleasure find
The savage and the tender
Some social join and leagues combine
Some solitary wander.
Avaunt, away! the cruel sway
Tyrannic man's dominion
The sportsman's joy, the murdering cry
The fluttering gory pinion.

But, Peggy dear, the evening's clear
Thick flies the skimming swallow
The sky is blue the fields in view
All fading – green and yellow.
Come let us stray our gladsome way
And view the charms of nature
The rustling corn, the fruited thorn
And every happy creature.

We'll gently walk and sweetly talk
Till the silent moon shine clearly
I'll grasp thy waist and, fondly pressed
Swear how I love thee dearly.
Not vernal showers to budding flowers
Not autumn to the farmer
So dear can be as thou to me
My fair, my lovely charmer.

Now Westlin Winds

18

Old Words

Traditional Scottish

Slowly and melodically
Harp
mf

pp
mf

cresc.
f
mp

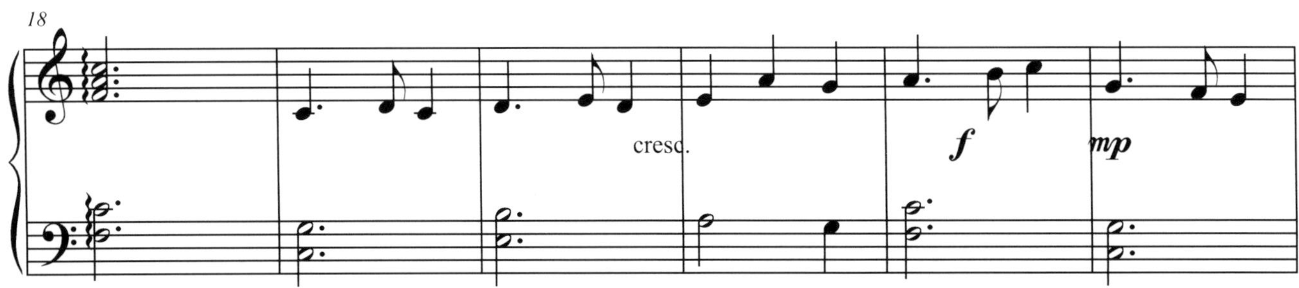

24
decresc.
p
mf
30
cresc.
f
mf
decresc.
36
pp
mf
42
48
21

54
a tempo
cresc.
rit.
f
mf

60
rit.
decresc.
pp

Soraidh Bhuam Gu Barraidh

Scottish Traditional, arr. SHR

Moderate 4 or slow 2

Harp

THE YELLOW-HAIRED LADDIE

The maidens are smiling in rocky Glencoe
The clansmen are arming to rush on the foe
Their banners are streaming as forth leaves the clan
And the yellow-haired laddie is first in the band

The pibroch is kindling their hearts to the war
Camerons slogans are heard from afar
They close for the struggle where many shall fall
And the yellow-haired laddie is the foremost of all

He towers on the wave like a wild rolling tide
No kinsman of valiance will stand by his side
The Camerons gather around him alone
He heeds not the danger and fear is unknown

The plumes o' his bonnet are seen in the fight
Those beacons of valour they light with his sight
But his sword and his claymore are greater distressed
For the plumes o' his bonnet now lie in the dust

The maidens are weeping in rocky Glencoe
From warriors' eyelids those bitter tears flow
Where, tell me where, is our chieftain so dear?
And the yellow-haired laddie lies low on the brae.

The Yellow-Haired Laddie

Traditional Scottish

Harp

Urnaigh A 'Bhan-Thigreach

rit.
p

UNIQUELY INTERESTING MUSIC!